Usborne Nat[ure]

Trees

Usborne Naturetrail
Trees

Laura Howell

Designed by
Laura Hammonds, Reuben Barrance,
Michael Hill and Kate Rimmer

Consultant: Derek Patch, Tree Advice Trust

Edited by Kirsteen Rogers

Internet links

There are lots of websites with information and activities for nature lovers. At the Usborne Quicklinks website we have provided links to some great sites where you can:

* explore a virtual wood and find out how trees are planted
* create your own online nature diary
* enter competitions and win prizes
* find the oldest trees growing near your home
* investigate how woods provide shelter and food for animals
* use an online identification guide to British trees
* see photos of woodland creatures, and spot them on a webcam
* find ideas for science and craft activities with trees and leaves

For links to these sites, go to the Usborne Quicklinks website at www.usborne.com/quicklinks and enter the keywords "naturetrail trees".

CONTENTS

Looking at trees

A closer look

From flowers to seeds

Life in a tree

Trees to spot

Trees and people

Green giants

Trees are some of nature's most amazing creations. When you see a mature tree, you're looking not only at a large plant, but at a living thing that may have existed before your grandparents' grandparents were born, a giant that came from a seed no bigger than your nose.

Supported by its thick, woody trunk, an English oak tree can grow up to 23m (75ft) and live for over 200 years.

What makes a tree a tree?

In many ways, a tree is just like any other plant. If you compare, say, an oak tree and a daisy, you can see why. Both of them have roots below the ground and green leaves above (for part of the time, anyway). Both once grew from seeds and they both grow flowers and fruits, too.

By comparison, a daisy plant grows to about 10cm (4in) each year then dies back to its roots. Its whole life is over in a few years.

So, what does make trees trees? Firstly, they have woody trunks rather than fleshy stems, and they have branches growing from them. Secondly, trees can usually grow much, much bigger than other plants. Although there isn't an official minimum height to qualify, plants aren't usually called trees unless they can grow at least 6m (20ft) tall.

Thirdly, and most impressively, trees can live longer than any animal or any other plant on the planet. You can watch a poppy grow and die in a year, but an oak tree might live beyond its 600th birthday. The oldest known tree in the world is over 4,800 years old, and still growing.

Life-support machines

At first glance, trees may not appear to do much, but they may be very busy: sheltering animals, or feeding them with their fruits and seeds, protecting the soil with their roots, cleaning the air with their leaves... their influence is everywhere. If you sit on a wooden bench to eat an apple and read a book, every one of those things was once part of a tree. In fact, without trees, life as you know it just couldn't exist.

DID YOU KNOW?
Trees first appeared on Earth about 370 million years ago. In time, thick forests grew over nearly all the land but now, trees cover less than one third of it. Over 100,000 different kinds of trees have been identified so far.

Not just a pretty sight, forests like this one provide homes for thousands of birds and other animals.

Western hemlock leaves and cone

There's a clear difference between a typical conifer (above) and a typical broadleaf (below).

Tree types

No matter how different they look, almost all trees belong to one of two groups: broadleaves or conifers. Conifer trees grow cones containing seeds, and their leaves are mostly needle-like or small and scaly. The leaves of broadleaved trees, on the other hand, tend to be wide and flat.

Broadleaves

Many, though not all, broadleaves are deciduous, which means they lose their leaves in autumn. The leaves' flat surfaces help them soak up plenty of sunlight, but water is quickly lost into the air, in the same way as large, shallow puddles dry up more quickly than smaller, deeper ones after a shower.

Broadleaves, like this maple, often turn spectacular colours in autumn.

Tropical trees are broadleaves that only grow in very hot, damp areas such as rainforests and swamps, so you won't see them in Europe. All trees need sunlight and water to grow. Having access to so much of both of these allows tropical trees to grow fast and large, often crowding very close together as they fight for space.

Many tropical trees provide foods, including the cacao pods used to make chocolate.

 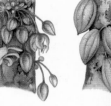

Cacao tree flowers...   ...ripen into cacao pods.

The rainforest contains so many trees, they have to grow in layers. The tallest ones dwarf their neighbours...

...which in turn look down on the lowest level. With so many trees above, the forest floor is often as dark as night.

DID YOU KNOW?
Rainforests cover only 6% of the land on Earth, yet they're home to two-thirds of all its plant and animal species.

Palm trees also prefer hot weather, but need less moisture than tropical trees. If you live in Britain, you'll rarely see palms growing outside, although they can manage well indoors as house plants. You'll know a palm when you see one because its large leaves usually grow in a bunch at the top of the trunk.

No side branches

Many palm trees have bendy trunks, so they don't break in severe tropical storms.

Conifers

The most familiar kinds of conifers are the spiky ones you see at Christmas or in pictures of snowy scenes. There are only about 600 types of conifer, compared with tens of thousands of broadleaves, but they're found almost worldwide, especially in dry or cold areas where broadleaves can't survive.

Conifers can be most easily recognized by their thin, needly leaves or sturdy little scales. Most are evergreens, which shed leaves throughout the year, instead of all in one go in autumn. The trees are usually tall and cone- or rocket-shaped, although some develop a round top like a broadleaved tree. Conifers have cones with seeds inside them. The word comes from Latin, meaning "cone carrying".

Even ice and snow are no match for these tough, waxy conifer needles.

Western red cedar

Some conifers have sprays of small, scale-like leaves.

Pine cone

Many types of cones are brown and woody.

Keep an eye out for these two common shapes of conifer trees.

Western hemlock

Shore pine

As they get older, many conifers lose their lower branches.

One of a kind

Some trees are much harder to categorize and don't really belong to conifers or broadleaves. Ginkgo trees, also known as maidenhair trees, are the only living relatives of a type of tree that first appeared on Earth over 250 million years ago. Ginkgoes used to grow only in China, but now you might see them in parks or planted along streets all over the world.

DID YOU KNOW?
Ginkgo trees have changed so little over time that if you put a million-year-old fossilized imprint of one next to a fresh leaf, they would look very similar.

Fossilized ginkgo leaf

A ginkgo leaf is a distinctive fan shape, and very soft to touch.

Ginkgo fruits look like small, yellow plums.

The leaves turn a rich yellow in autumn before falling.

Tree or shrub?

Trees that grow in tough conditions, or are deliberately trimmed, sometimes stay quite small. These smaller, bushy trees are often known as shrubs, especially if they have several stems branching from near the ground. Most shrubs are broadleaved, but there are a few shrubs that are conifers, too. Some small, woody plants, such as lavender, are also called shrubs.

Juniper can be a tree or a shrub, depending whether it's more or less than 6m (20ft).

Oak buds grow
in lumpy clumps.

Aspen

Rowan

An aspen leaf is one
single piece, while a
rowan leaf has lots
of small leaflets.

Looking for clues

When you're out and about, stop and look at the trees around you. You may be able to tell quite easily whether they're broadleaves or conifers, but you'll need more clues to find out exactly what kind of trees they are. Fortunately, there's always something that'll help you find a tree's identity.

Spring and summer

Spring is the time of year when buds are unfurling into flowers and fresh, young leaves. Early in the season, get in close and examine the buds before they open. Are they sticky, scaly, hairy, or bumpy? This is also the only time you can see a tree's flowers, so take the opportunity to have a good look. Some are like garden flowers, with soft petals and a sweet scent, while others are dull and lumpy, with no particular smell at all.

In the summer's heat, the flowers die off but the leaves keep developing. As well as obvious things like their size and shape, notice how they're arranged on the twig, and whether they grow in ones or groups.

Cherry trees in spring look
almost as if they're made
of nothing but flowers.

Autumn and winter

In autumn, the days get shorter and many trees lose their leaves. Luckily, though, there's something new to spot: fruits and nuts. These come in many shapes and sizes, from bead-like berries and tough nuts to woody cones. Look for them on the ground, being eaten by birds, or even up above, being blown through the air.

Not all fruits can be eaten. These larch cones are fruits, but you wouldn't want to take a bite.

Fruits aren't always soft and fleshy – these tough acorns are oak tree fruits.

A bare tree in winter might look dead, but it's just "sleeping" through the cold weather. Now's the perfect time to stand back and look at the tree's overall shape.

Stripped of its leafy coat, the trunks and branches of this common alder are easy to see.

You can recognize a Scots pine tree by its reddish or pinky-grey upper bark that flakes off in "plates".

Finally, remember that any season is good for taking a close look at a tree's bark.

Silver birch bark feels smooth to the touch, and has a subtle silvery sheen.

HANDY HINTS

To help you choose
a field guide:
• Look up a tree
you already know.
Does the picture
look like the tree?
• Are the words
easy to read?
• Are there pictures
of flowers, fruits,
bark and buds as
well as leaves?

Using a field guide

Imagine you're setting out into the countryside (or town, or park, or garden) hoping to identify each tree you see. The most useful thing to take along is a field guide – a book of bite-sized facts about all kinds of trees. Most guides separate broadleaves from conifers, then arrange trees in smaller family groups, based on features such as the shape and arrangement of their leaves.

Below, you can see the kind of information you will find in a typical field guide, although it varies from book to book. There's a short field guide at the back of this book, starting on page 60.

Most field guides show
a leaf and a flower. Some
show a picture of the
whole tree and a close-up
of its bark, too.

HORSE CHESTNUT

Species: *Aesculus hippocastanum*
Family: *Hippocastanaceae*
Habitat: Mountain woods

This is where the tree
usually grows wild.

A tree's Latin scientific
names may not be the
ones you know them by.

Height:
30m (100ft)

This is the maximum
height an adult tree
would normally reach.

White petals with
yellow or, later,
pink patches

Prickly fruit with
conkers inside

Vital statistics

A good field guide will tell you how tall a tree can grow, so it's useful to know the height of a particular tree you've seen. Forget ladders and enormous tape measures, all you need is a friend and a calculator, or a good head for sums.

Before you start, find out exactly how tall your friend is. Ask him or her to stand next to the tree you want to measure, then walk a little way away and look carefully. Imagine lots of copies of your friend, one above the other. How many of them do you think it would take to reach the top of the tree? You can then multiply this number by your friend's height to estimate the height of the tree.

To measure the distance around a tree's trunk (its girth, in tree-speak), put a tape measure around the trunk at your chin height. If a tree has several trunks, measure its thickest one.

If your friend is 1.5m (5ft) tall, and the tree is roughly six times taller, the tree is about 9m (30ft) tall.

To measure a very thick trunk, give a friend one end of the tape and walk around the tree with the other until you meet.

You could jot down notes about trees and draw sketches of them, so if you see a tree you don't know and haven't got a field guide, you can look it up later.

HANDY HINTS
Useful details to note:
• Where the tree was
• Its height
• Shape of leaves
• Appearance of any buds, flowers or fruit

Life begins

Even the mightiest tree starts life as a fragile seedling and growing up is slow, hard work. Here you can read the story of a young sycamore tree, but you'll find that most trees grow in a similar way.

From seed to seedling

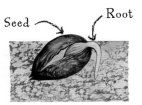

Seed   Root

1. A tree starts to grow in spring from a seed. With the help of food stored inside it, the seed sends down a root into the soil to suck up water and minerals, which it needs so it can grow.

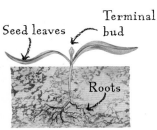

Seed leaves   Terminal bud   Roots

2. A tiny shoot pushes its way up out of the seed towards the light. Two fleshy leaves unfurl, with a bud in between. These seed leaves are usually shaped differently from the tree's normal ones. The bud at the tip of a shoot is the terminal bud.

Leaves   Seed leaves

3. The seedling grows, using food stored in the seed. Soon the bud opens and the real leaves unfurl. When they're no longer needed, the seed leaves die. During the summer, a bud forms at the base of each leaf. The roots get longer, sprouting smaller side roots, too.

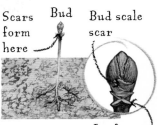

Scars form here   Bud   Bud scale scar   Leaf scar

4. In autumn, the leaves change colour and drop off, leaving a mark called a scar on the stem. The buds at the end of the shoot are ready to open up next spring.

Getting stronger

In the second spring of the seedling's life, its buds open, making new leaves and a new shoot. Buds on the stem may develop into side shoots. When autumn returns, the leaves drop off. You'll see these same things happening year after year.

Each year, the seedling's stem becomes thicker and taller and develops more side shoots and leaves. Eventually, the stem becomes a trunk, and the side shoots grow into branches. Instead of a fragile plant, it's now a young tree, but there's still lots more growing to do...

1. This seedling is in its first growing season.

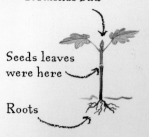

Terminal bud

Seeds leaves were here

Roots

2. This seedling is in its second growing season.

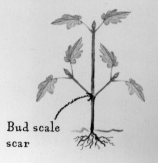

Bud scale scar

3. This seedling is in its third growing season.

Bud scale scar

This shoot is no longer than a pencil, but many, many years from now it will be a giant sycamore tree.

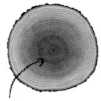

In the centre of the tree is heartwood. This is the oldest part, made mostly of dead water-carrying tubes.

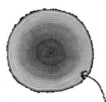

Around the heartwood is the sapwood, which brings water up from the roots as a liquid called sap.

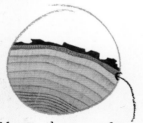

Next to the sapwood is a layer of inner bark, which carries food made in the leaves to the rest of the tree.

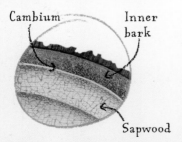

Cambium   Inner bark

Sapwood

Both sapwood and inner bark are made by a thin layer called cambium. It is sandwiched between them.

Inside the trunk

Apart from the growth you can see at the tips of stems and shoots, a tree is busy growing on the inside, too. A very thin layer, so thin you'd hardly see it, makes tubes that carry water up and down the tree. Without these, the tree would die. This layer, called cambium, creates new tubes every spring and summer – so the trunk gets slowly thicker, year by year.

As the tree ages, the tubes harden and die, making the woody rings you can see in a tree stump. There's one for each year of its life.

Peculiar palms

Compared with other trees, palms grow in an unusual way. They have no cambium layer, just clumps of food- and water-carrying tubes around a pithy core. After a palm reaches its adult girth, the only growth is at the top of the trunk.

The inside of a palm is more like the inside of a flower stem than a tree trunk.

Palm trunk

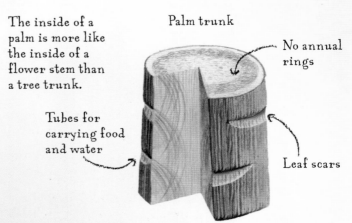

No annual rings

Tubes for carrying food and water

Leaf scars

Growing branches

Branches grow longer each year, but the base of a branch always stays the same height above the ground, no matter how tall the tree is. This is because the trunk and branches only extend at their ends. It would be the same if you only grew at the top of your head and tips of your fingers: your shoulders would always be the same distance from the floor.

Side branches start to grow.

As the tree grows wider and taller, so the branches become wider and longer.

Maples like this need a super-strong trunk to bear the colossal weight of such wide and heavy branches.

A tree that's reached its full height doesn't get any taller, but it does keep getting wider. The girth of a tree trunk usually increases by about 2.5cm (1in) a year. Although this kind of growth isn't as easy to see as the sprouting twigs and buds, it's just as important. Trees are so heavy on top, they need strong, thick trunks to keep them from collapsing under the weight of their own branches and leaves.

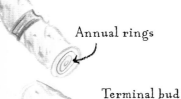

Annual rings

Terminal bud

Bud scale scar shows
where the last year's
leading bud grew.

If you cut a twig in two,
the number of rings
inside should match the
number of bud scale
scars on the outside.

Annual rings

If you look at a tree stump, you'll
see patterns of rings all the way
across, usually one light and one dark
each year. These patterns are called
annual rings, because the tree makes a
new one every year as its trunk expands.

Counting the number of annual rings in
a tree stump will tell you how old the tree
was when it was cut down. This works
for fallen branches too, as they also have
annual rings inside. Even twigs have them.

This dent shows that
the tree was damaged,
a long time ago.

Reading rings

The wider one annual ring is, the more the tree
grew in that year, and this is usually linked to
the weather in that growing season. It's
amazing to think that just by looking
at a tree ring, you can tell
whether there was a very
cold year a century ago.

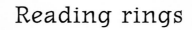

A year with
lots of growth

A year with
little growth

Slow growth years
are usually caused by
wet, chilly weather.

The shape and position of annual rings can reveal more secrets about the history of any tree stump you find. On the right, you can see some examples of ring patterns you might spot.

No two trees have exactly the same shapes and patterns of annual rings.

These rings have a dimple on one side, which means a branch was once growing there.

This tree grew unevenly, maybe because one side was more sheltered than the other, or because the wind bent the tree as it grew.

The first ten years of this tree's life were hard-going, but it started to grow more strongly after that.

You can also look at the light and dark rings. The light layer is early wood, formed in spring when the tree is growing quickly. The dark layer is late wood, made when growth slows down in summer. You can sometimes see these light and dark patterns as stripes in wooden planks, floorboards or fence panels.

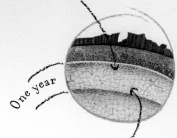

Late growth layer

One year

Early growth layer

A tree's bark can be as distinctive as its leaves or fruits. Look closely, and feel its surface.

Birch bark peels off in wispy strips.

London plane bark flakes into large scales on older trees.

The bark of beech trees is thin and smooth.

Bark

Bark may seem a bit boring compared with flowers or leaves, but it's one of a tree's most vital parts. You could think of bark as the tree's skin, protecting its insides from damage, just as your skin protects you.

Without bark, the tree's inner parts would be in danger from pests and diseases, or could dry out and die. The bark of some trees, such as giant sequoia, can even help protect them from the intense heat of forest fires.

A thick skin

Bark is made of two layers – the outer bark, which is what you can see, and an inner bark layer underneath that grows every year. The thickness of bark can vary widely from one type of tree to another. Beech trees rely on only 1cm (0.5in) or so of bark for protection, whereas some redwoods are shielded by a generous 30cm (1ft) of the stuff.

A tree's outer bark is dead, so it can't expand as the trunk grows. Young trees have a covering of thin, smooth bark. But, as the tree matures, this splits and cracks and eventually flakes or peels off revealing a new layer. Noticing the colour and texture of a tree's bark can help you look it up in a field guide.

Holey wood

If you spot big holes in a tree's bark, they may well have been made by animals. Bark has natural, small holes of its own, too. These allow the tree to "breathe", taking in air from all around. Air holes are easiest to see on smooth bark, and often look like pale blisters or thin strips.

These rough bands in cherry bark are its "breathing holes".

You can identify a paper-bark maple tree by its chocolatey brown bark that peels off in wafer-thin whorls and frills.

Bark rubbing

If you'd like to keep a record of the different types of bark you've seen, you could make a bark rubbing. Here are two different methods to try.

1. This method is the simplest. Place some plain paper on the bark and rub on it with a wax crayon to make an impression of the bark's texture.

2. Put the paper on the bark and rub over it with a plain wax candle. At home, brush over it with poster paint. The bark pattern will remain white.

Roots

It's easy to forget that a huge part of any tree is hidden away in the earth. Roots anchor the tree firmly in the ground and, most importantly, soak up water and goodness from the soil – sometimes hundreds of litres in a day. They also serve as a food store.

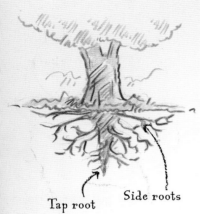

Tap root   Side roots

Many trees have a thick, main root, called a tap root, that may grow straight down, deeper than any other. Smaller side roots sprout from it, spreading out to form a tangled mesh just below the soil's surface. These in turn develop rootlets, which are smaller and thinner still. The roots have protective tips that force through the soil as the roots lengthen. Every year, rootlets grow millions of tiny hairs that suck in water and goodness from the soil. This is then drawn up through the roots, into the trunk and to the rest of the tree.

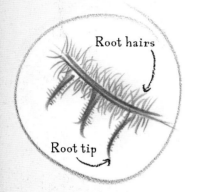

Root hairs

Root tip

Life in the soil

Armies of creepy crawlies live unseen around a tree's roots. The young larvae of many insects are pests, feeding on the fresh growing rootlets. But there are helpful animals too: earthworms wriggle down from the surface, drawing air and dead leaves into the soil as they burrow. This puts goodness back into the soil, which in turn helps to keep the trees healthy.

Size and strength

A tree's roots don't go as deep as you might think. Even the tap roots of most large trees are no deeper than 1.5m (5ft). The really surprising thing is how far out they spread. Like branches, roots can grow longer and thicker each year. Most side roots lie within 1m (3ft) of the soil surface, but they can spread to form a vast web that's even wider than the tree is tall.

Even the strongest roots can't always stand up to a howling gale. Occasionally you might find a tree that's been uprooted in a storm, especially in woods. If you do, it can be an ideal opportunity to get close for a really good look.

If a growing root reaches an obstacle, such as a stone, it just grows around it.

Old roots become tough and woody, creating a wide, stiff "net" to hold the tree in place.

This elm's roots were torn when it fell. Most of them are still left underground.

Two-coloured leaves, like this holly, are called variegated leaves. They're quite rare.

A goat willow's oval leaves are dark green and wrinkly on top, but underneath they're grey-green and rough.

Looking at leaves

There's no better way to start getting to know a tree than by looking at and touching its leaves. The more you notice about a tree's leaves, the easier it will be to look it up in a field guide.

Lift a leaf up, run your finger around its edge, and stroke its surface. How does it feel? New leaves, fresh from the bud, are as soft and smooth as silk, while older ones might be leathery or tough. Some feel crinkly, or sticky, or have sharp prickles or downy hairs.

What does the leaf look like? Is it a broadleaf or a needle, large or small, droopy or firm? What about the length, shape and colour of its stalk?

A leaf can be almost any shade of green, but keep an eye open for subtle or bright reds and yellows, pinks and purples, oranges, greys and browns.

These newly opened beech leaves have baby-soft hairs, which will disappear as they get older.

What are leaves for?

Leaves have the important job of making food to keep the tree alive. Chlorophyll, the chemical that makes leaves green, soaks up sunlight. The leaf then uses energy from the sunlight to combine water with carbon dioxide gas from the air, and turn it into nourishing, sugary sap for the tree. This process also makes oxygen, the gas in the air that you breathe, so leaves are very important for people and animals, too.

If you look closely at a leaf, you'll see a network of veins spreading across it. Water travels up through root, trunk, branch and twig from the soil, then through the veins into the leaves. The veins then take sap back to the tree's food transport system. The liquid-filled veins also keep the leaves firm, just as your skeleton stops your body from being soft and floppy.

A leaf's flat surface acts like a solar panel, absorbing sunlight.

The Sun only shines on the top, so many leaves are pale underneath.

DID YOU KNOW?

You may have seen leaves dancing in the breeze, but they can move on their own, too. Very, very slowly, a leaf turns so it's in the best position to face the Sun.

If you put a plant on a windowsill, you'll notice its leaves start pointing to the light after a few days.

The thickest vein is in the middle. Lots of smaller veins branch off it.

Silver maple leaf

A tough stem attaches the leaf to the twig.

Water from the trunk gets into the veins through the stem.

The veins in conifer needles run straight along the leaf, but they are difficult to see.

Broadleaf shapes

The simplest broadleaf shape is called a simple leaf, and it's just a single piece. Simple leaves can be round or oval, heart-shaped or slim, with edges that are ragged, toothed (jagged) or smooth.

Compound leaves are made up of smaller leafy parts known as leaflets. At first glance, they can look like a cluster of simple leaves, but they're all attached to the twig by the same stalk. Leaflets often grow in pairs, either opposite their partners, or slightly offset, but some sprout from a middle point like fingers on a hand.

Many of the biggest leaves in the world are compound, including giant African raffia palms which, at a monstrous 25m (82ft), can grow to the length of a blue whale.

A lime's simple leaves are heart-shaped.

The edge of a lobed leaf wanders in and out in a wavy shape.

Leaves such as this sweet chestnut have a zigzag edge like a saw.

A smooth-edged leaf like this magnolia is called an entire or whole leaf.

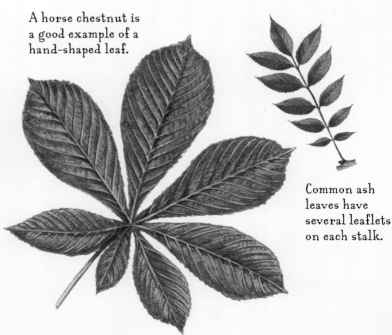

A horse chestnut is a good example of a hand-shaped leaf.

Common ash leaves have several leaflets on each stalk.

Cedars have short needles which grow mainly in circular clusters called rosettes.

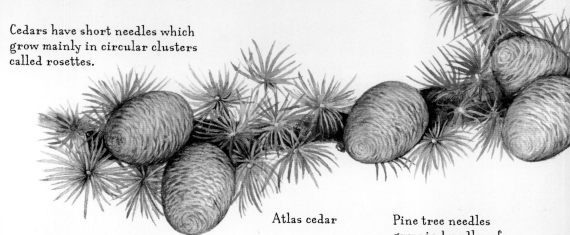

Atlas cedar

Pine tree needles grow in bundles of two, three or five.

Scots pine (twos)

Needles and scales

Almost all conifer leaves are either slim needles or stubby scales, but you'll still find plenty of variety. Just like broadleaves, they grow in different arrangements, shapes and sizes. The world's largest tree, the giant sequoia, has scales that are smaller than your fingernail.

The branches and twigs of monkey puzzle trees are covered with overlapping rows of hard, pointy scales.

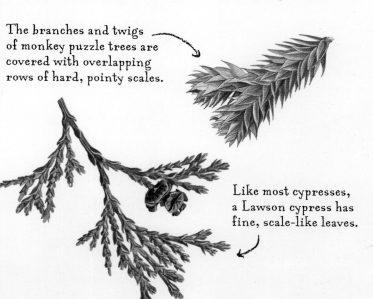

Like most cypresses, a Lawson cypress has fine, scale-like leaves.

Monterey pine (threes)

Swiss stone pine (fives)

Sycamore

Maple

Autumn leaves

You'll know deciduous trees are preparing for winter when their leaves start to change. As the autumn days get shorter and colder, the chlorophyll breaks down, and so the green fades, giving way to red, yellow and orange. As well as creating one of the most breathtaking displays in the treespotters' calendar, autumn also gives you a chance to do some activities with fallen leaves you've collected from the ground.

The chemicals that made these rich autumn shades were in the leaves all along, but were hidden by green chlorophyll.

English oak

Horse chestnut

Beech

Rowan

Leaves of northern red oak trees turn reddish brown in autumn.

A leaf scrapbook

A scrapbook filled with pressed
autumn leaves can be a decorative
and handy reminder of the
trees you've seen.

Next to each leaf you could
make a note of where and
when you found it, and
what type of leaf it is.

1. Collect some fallen leaves
and wipe off any water or
dirt. You'll need sheets of
blotting or tissue paper and
a stack of heavy books, too.

2. Place each leaf between
two pieces of paper and put
them in the back of a book.
Pile the other books on top
and leave for a few weeks.

3. Carefully stick your
pressed leaves into a
scrapbook with tape, and
write all the details you
know next to each one.

Leaf skeletons

In fine weather, fallen leaves sometimes
dry out and crumble away, leaving behind
delicate, lacy skeletons of stems and veins.
If you look on the ground in winter, you
might find part of a leaf skeleton. You may
even find a whole one that's survived. If
not, you can create a similar effect by
taking a rubbing from a clean, fallen
leaf. Put a piece of paper over the
top, and rub over the paper
with a pencil crayon.

You could keep a colourful
record of the leaves you've
collected by making a
notebook of rubbings.

Like this wych elm, many broadleaved trees have rounded crowns.

The branch ends of "weeping" trees bend towards the ground.

Rocket-like shapes are more common among conifers than broadleaved trees.

A Lombardy poplar is one of the few broadleaf trees with a tall, narrow crown.

Tree shapes

You can often identify a tree by looking at its overall shape. To get a good idea of the shape of a tree, it's best to look at it from a slight distance, so you can get the whole tree in view.

Is it tall and slender, or stubby and wide? Do its branches sweep dramatically upwards or droop gracefully down? Or maybe they stick scarecrow-like straight out to the sides?

A tree's shape can help it make the most of the conditions it grows in. Many trees in sunny places have deep crowns – that is, their branches and leaves extend to ground level. They have plenty of leaves to soak up as much sunlight as they can. In woodland, where trees have to compete for space and light, the lower branches tend to die because there is too much shade.

Dragon trees grow high up in the Canary Islands, where it is warm but often cloudy.

An umbrella-shaped crown soaks up sunlight from above.

The leafy canopy collects water from mist and cloud. It trickles down the branches, into the ground and to the roots.

32

Trees near the coast often grow bent and twisted, battered by waves or strong sea winds.

Odd shapes

Have you ever noticed that a few trees have weird shapes compared to others of their kind? Lots of things can affect a tree's shape, including the weather, where it's growing, and other trees nearby.

Growing alone, a tree such as this oak is free to spread out.

Closer together, these oaks can only grow upwards, so they're tall and thin.

Trees growing on mountains are often left small and stubby by the cold, dry winds.

A coppiced tree, growing new shoots

Chopping and changing

Sometimes, a tree's shape has been changed on purpose. Cutting a young tree down to a stump, and so allowing it to make lots of healthy new shoots, is called coppicing. Cutting its branches off near the trunk is called pollarding. This is done to control a tree's height. You may see roadside trees that have been pollarded to stop them from growing too big.

Newly pollarded trees often look like twiggy trunks.

33

Budding growth

In winter, many trees seem dead and bare, but if you look closely you can see buds on their twigs and branches. These contain the furled-up beginnings of leaves, flowers and shoots, waiting to burst into life in spring. It's often possible to tell what type a tree is just by looking at its buds, which can be as distinctive as its leaves or crown shape. You could see how many trees you can identify using the bud guide on pages 70-71.

A sycamore bud splits open to reveal fresh new leaves, which will slowly unfurl over a day or two.

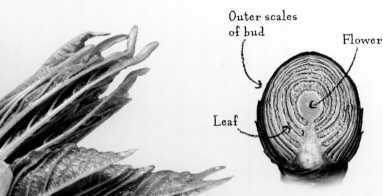

Outer scales of bud

Flower

Leaf

If you cut a bud in half, you'd see many tightly packed layers.

The fine hairs on magnolia buds are as soft as a kitten's fur.

Most buds have thick, overlapping scales to protect the delicate shoot inside from the cold and from greedy insects. In places where there's not much rain in winter, the bud scales also stop the shoot from drying out. Some buds don't have scales at all – instead, their unopened leaves are protected by a thick covering of downy hair.

34

How buds grow

In spring, when the weather warms up, a new shoot swells and breaks open a bud's protective scales. At the end of the growing season, every shoot will have a new bud at the tip, ready for next year.

Undeveloped twig

Side buds will become shoots.

This horse chestnut twig has sticky, brown buds growing in pairs on opposite sides of the twig.

Horseshoe-shaped leaf scar has a row of black dots.

If this terminal bud is damaged, the bud next to it will become the new leading bud.

Bud scale scar, left behind by last year's leading bud

The main twig is three years old (you can tell by counting its bud scale scars). The side twig is two years old.

You don't have to wait until spring comes to see a bud open up. You could take a twig cutting in early January, put it in water and watch the buds open on your windowsill. Pussy willow, birch, horse chestnut and forsythia are the best trees to do this with.

NEED TO KNOW
Always ask a tree's owner before cutting: and clip the twig – don't snap it off. This avoids the tree being injured unnecessarily.

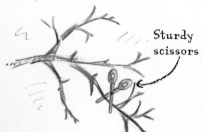

Sturdy scissors

1. Find a healthy adult tree and take your cutting. A 25cm (10in) twig is enough.

2. Put the cutting in a jam jar of water and leave it in a sunny place indoors.

3. Keep the water to the same level. In a few weeks, the buds will start to open.

Ash flowers are tiny purple bobbles. You have to look really closely to spot them.

Magnolias, on the other hand, are hard to miss. They can be big and showy, the size of a fist, with a fresh, sweet fragrance.

Flowers

People often think of flowers and trees as separate sorts of plants, yet all trees make flowers. Without them, they couldn't create seeds to grow into new trees. The way a flower looks and grows depends on the type of tree it's from. Some are big and fancy, and others are so tiny you'd barely know they were flowers at all.

Flowers have male and female parts. Their male bits, called stamens, make powdery pollen, and their female bits, called ovaries, have tiny eggs inside. When pollen reaches the eggs in another flower, the flower is fertilized. It then loses its petals and becomes a fruit with one or more seeds inside.

DID YOU KNOW?

Fig flowers might be the oddest of all tree flowers. They grow inside an unusual pod, which later becomes the tree's fruit.

Fig flowers

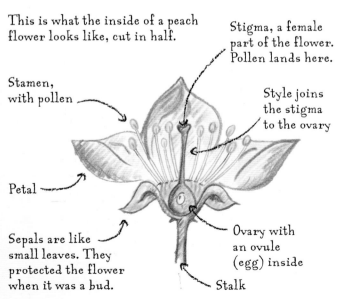

This is what the inside of a peach flower looks like, cut in half.

Stamen, with pollen

Petal

Sepals are like small leaves. They protected the flower when it was a bud.

Stigma, a female part of the flower. Pollen lands here.

Style joins the stigma to the ovary

Ovary with an ovule (egg) inside

Stalk

Flower types

There are three ways that tree flowers grow. Many trees, including conifers, have separate male and female flowers growing on the same tree. Some, such as apples and plums, keep all their male and female bits together in every flower. A few types of trees, such as ash and yew, have their male and female flowers on different trees.

Every one of these apple blossoms has both male and female parts.

It's quite common for trees to have clusters of dangly flowers called catkins. These can be male or female. If you find a tree with catkins and dumpy little flowers at the end of each twig, the catkin is usually male and the other flower is female.

Male flower   Female flower

Holly has male and female flowers on separate trees.

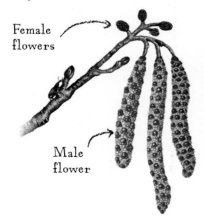

Female flowers

Male flower

Each of the red blobs on these dangling male alder catkins is actually an individual flower.

Style

Stamen

You have to get in close to see a hawthorn flower's stamens and style.

Pollen on the move

Growing flowers is only the first part of making seeds. The next challenge a tree faces is how to spread its pollen from flower to flower. Unless this happens, no fruits can grow.

Pollen carriers

Many flowers "hire" insects to do this vital job. Flowers attract their attention with bright colours or a strong perfume, and many contain a sweet liquid called nectar which insects love to drink.

 The point of this isn't to feed the insects, though – it's to bribe them to land, so that pollen sticks to their bodies. Although many trees use bees to move their pollen, there are some trees whose pollen is carried by birds, bats or other furry creatures.

A passing bee, lured by the scent, lands on the apple blossom.

The bee clambers into the flower to drink nectar. Pollen sticks to its body.

The bee flies away to another flower, where the pollen rubs off the bee, onto the flower's stigma.

An Australian honey possum gets a dusting of pollen as it feeds on nectar in these gum tree flowers.

Pretty versus plain

Pollen carriers don't arrive at particular flowers by chance. Many insects have a favourite flower type, usually because of its colour or scent. You can see this for yourself by watching particular tree flowers and noticing what comes to visit.

Butterflies and birds are often attracted to red, pink or purple flowers.

Some trees don't have bright petals, perfume or nectar to offer, so insects tend not to visit them. But they don't need to attract animals, though, as their pollen is spread by the wind. The dangling catkins are covered in pollen, which wafts away as they jiggle in the breeze.

Pollen blows from male crack willow's flowers to the female ones.

Female crack willow flowers

From bee to you

When pollen from one tree lands on the stigmas of flowers on another one, fruits start to develop. Every year on fruit farms all over the world, millions of bees are brought in hives into orchards, to help spread large quantities of pollen and make sure that plenty of fruit can be produced.

Without pollen carriers you wouldn't find these items on the supermarket shelves.

Apples

Almonds

Coffee beans

Fruits and seeds

Soon after a flower has been fertilized with pollen, its petals drop off. Inside the ovary the fertilized ovule slowly turns into a seed, while outer layers develop to form a fruit.

Each of these cherries has a stone inside that could eventually become a new cherry tree.

An apple and a prickly conker case are both fruits. But no matter how different fruits look from each other, their job is the same. They protect the seeds they carry and help them get to a place where they can grow into new trees.

DID YOU KNOW?
Durians, which grow in Asia, are among the world's strangest fruits. They can grow as big as footballs, are covered in spikes, and give off a foul stink. Yet many people find their custard-like flesh delicious.

Fertilized peach blossom...

Petals will fall off

Stem

Ovule

The fertilized ovule grows into a seed.

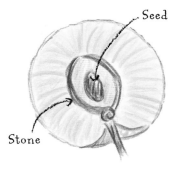

... becomes a ripe, juicy peach.

Seed

Stone

The fleshy layer grows from the stem and the ovary becomes a stone.

Broadleaf fruits

Broadleaf fruits come in a huge range of shapes and sizes. Many are soft, whole fruits, such as apples, peaches, cherries and plums, but they can also take the form of berries and pods. Some fruits hold just one big seed, and others have more.

They may look very different, but all these fruits come from broadleaved trees.

Wych elm

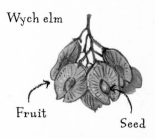

Fruit

Seed

Rowan

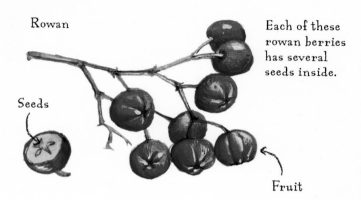

Each of these rowan berries has several seeds inside.

Seeds

Fruit

Plane

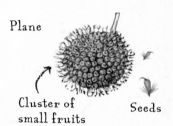

Cluster of small fruits

Seeds

Some trees, such as hazels, grow nuts instead of fruits. But nuts are a type of fruit, too. It's just that they have a hard outer shell, which has to rot away or be peeled off or cracked open to let the seed out. Some have prickles or spikes to give extra protection.

Sweet chestnut

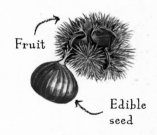

Fruit

Edible seed

Walnut   Fruit

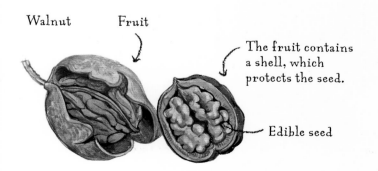

The fruit contains a shell, which protects the seed.

Edible seed

Oak

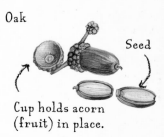

Seed

Cup holds acorn (fruit) in place.

Cones

Instead of being soft and tasty like broadleaf fruits, conifer fruits are tough, scaly cones. The scales act like armour, protecting the seeds inside. Cones develop from a tree's female flowers. Once a flower is fertilized, a cone develops and its scales harden and close up.

Over time, the cone gradually turns from green to brown. When it's ripe and ready, it releases its seeds, either by breaking up slowly on the branch, or by letting them drop before tumbling, empty, to the ground.

Some cones stay on the tree for a year, but others take two or more years to ripen. Some hang on the tree long after the seeds have dropped and occasionally cones fall too soon. This is good news for seed-hungry animals – and it also gives you an opportunity to collect fallen cones and take a closer look.

Douglas fir

Male flower

Female flower

1. Cones develop from the female flowers, which look like mini cones.

Young cone in summer

2. When a flower is fertilized, ovules become seeds inside a developing cone. At first, it's green.

Empty cone

3. Most mature cones are brown and hard. The scales open in warm, dry weather.

Pine cones shed their seeds over several years.

Seed

42

Cone shapes

Cones are more varied than you'd imagine. They can be as small as a pea or as long as your arm; long or round, smooth, knobbly, sticky or crinkly. A few don't even look like cones at all.

Cones can either grow alone or in bunches, like these pine cones.

Young Lawson cypress cones

Cedar of Lebanon cone

Norway spruce cone

Juniper and yew cones look just like berries.

Yew cones

Juniper cones

If it's cold, a cone stays tightly closed.

Hot, dry conditions make it open.

Weather forecasters

People used to say that cones could predict the weather, and there's some truth in that. Cones only open and drop their seeds when conditions are dry. If it starts to get too wet or cold, they close again. If you want to see this happen, just find a closed cone and put it near a hot radiator.

Scattering seeds

It's a tough life for a seed. Many of the fruits that contain them are ruined by insects or disease, or fall off the tree and die before they can ripen. The seeds that are lucky enough to be protected by undamaged and healthy fruits need to get away from the parent tree to find a spot of their own in which to grow. This is so they don't have to compete with the adult tree for water, space and light.

Of course, a seed stuck inside a fruit can't make its way out into the world alone: it needs to hitch a ride. That's why so many fruits, berries and nuts are juicy or delicious. Being eaten is one of the best possible ways to spread seeds.

If this squirrel buries the hazelnut to eat later and forgets where it's put it, the nut will have a chance to grow into a tree.

Tempted by the bright colours of the fruits, birds and other animals eat luscious rowan berries with seeds inside.

The bird flies away. It digests the fruit, but the seed comes out in its droppings, away from the tree, where it can grow into a new tree.

Wind power

Generally, trees that don't need animals to spread their pollen don't rely on them to spread their seeds, either. Their fruits often have fluffy "parachutes" or paper-thin "wings", which catch the wind, allowing them to spiral away through the air like mini helicopters.

Ash
(one wing)

Lime (one wing)

Several fruits

If you find any seeds like these on the ground, throw them into the air and watch how they spin down.

Sycamore fruits have two seeds and a pair of papery wings.

With their light, downy "parachutes", willow seeds can easily be carried away by wind or by water.

Willow

Sailing away

As you might expect, trees that grow near seas or rivers, such as coconut palms, use water to carry their seeds. Coconut fruits are hollow, so they float easily, despite their size. Some drift thousands of miles across the ocean before washing up on a shore where they can sprout.

Alder

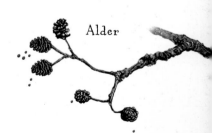

Look for alder trees near water. Each of their seeds has a natural oily coating, which keeps the seed afloat.

Growing a seedling

You can have a go at growing any seed you like. If one type of seed doesn't work, just try another.

One easy way to get a really good view of a growing tree is to grow seedlings of your own. You can plant pips and stones from any fresh, uncooked fruit. In autumn, you can try planting nuts and seeds you find outdoors.

Sweet chestnut

Seeds and stones from fruits such as apples, pears and cherries grow well – try growing one of each in separate pots. The amount of time it takes for a seed to grow depends on lots of things, including the time of year and the type of seed. If nothing has grown after six weeks or so, try again with different seeds.

Apple

Pear

Cherry

From one little acorn like this, a whole new tree begins.

Grow an acorn

For every seed you
plant you'll need:
a flowerpot, small
stones, saucer, soil or
compost, acorn* or
other seed/nut,
plastic bag, string
or large elastic bands

1. Put a handful of stones
in the bottom of the pot,
to help the water drain
properly. Place a saucer
underneath the pot.

2. Add soil or compost
until the pot is about
two-thirds full. Water
the soil until it is moist
but not soggy.

3. Lay the acorn on top
of the soil. Acorns need
plenty of room to grow,
so only plant one in
each pot.

4. Cover the acorn
with a layer of soil.
This layer should
be about as thick as
the acorn itself.

5. Tie the plastic bag over
the top. This keeps the
acorn moist, so you don't
need to water it. Put the
pot in a sunny place.

6. After a few weeks, a
seedling should appear.
When it does, take the bag
off and start watering the
seedling two or three times a
week to keep the soil damp.

7. In the summer, if you
can, move your seedling
outside in its pot. Carry
on watering it regularly.
In autumn, you could
plant it in the ground.

Water your seedling
before you plant it.

8. Dig a hole in the soil a
little bigger than the pot.
Gently lift the seedling
and the soil from the pot.
Plant them in the hole and
pat down the soil firmly.

*If you're growing an acorn, you need to start in the autumn. Plant an
acorn soon after you've collected it, otherwise the seed inside will dry out.
You can tell if an acorn is ripe because its cup will have fallen off.

Passing warblers snatch unsuspecting caterpillars off leaves, to feed to their young.

Woodpeckers peck holes in soft or rotten wood, and slurp out insects with their tongues.

A place to live

A large tree is nature's block of flats, with different creatures living and feeding at each level. Birds build nests in the branches. Squirrels and bats set up home in holes in the trunk, while small creatures live in the tree's basement, among its roots. Although all trees attract living things, woods and forests are the best places to see most of the ones shown here.

What's the attraction?

Trees offer food and shelter. There's plenty of space for nesting, and crevices to hide in. Vegetarian animals feast on seeds and berries, while meat-eaters take their pick of the many creepy crawlies that live on the leaves and bark, and even in the wood. Just one big tree can be home to thousands of living things.

Not all creatures you'll find around trees live there all the time – some visit to eat or rest, but live elsewhere. If you watch the comings and goings on a nearby tree, you might be able to work out who's a resident and who isn't.

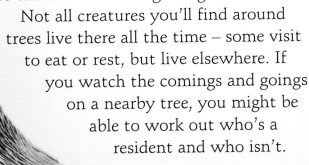

Hedgehogs snuffle through the dead leaves at the foot of a tree, looking for worms and insects to eat.

In the branches

The branches are mostly used by parent birds for building nests, so their babies are safe from hungry enemies on the ground. Look out for them flying back and forth to the tree with food, or listen for their calls and songs.

Perched on a branch, this robin is singing loudly to announce, "This is where I live - keep away!"

Squirrels sometimes build leafy nests, called dreys, among the branches.

Going down

Many insects live on a tree's trunk and bark, and holes in the trunk can make safe homes for birds and mammals, too. You might also see yellow or green crusty patches on a tree. These plant-like growths are called lichen. They are easily harmed by dirt in the air, such as vehicle exhaust, so the more lichen you find on a tree, the cleaner the air is.

Leafy lichen   Crust lichen

Various lichens grow on the bark of broadleaved trees.

Treecreepers run nimbly up and down tree trunks, hunting insects.

These red underwing moths' wing patterns are good camouflage on bark.

A hole at the foot of a tree might be the entrance to a badger's home, called a sett.

Snails nibble on plants growing under trees.

Life at the base of a tree

Lots of animals rest and hunt for food on the ground at the base of a tree. You're sometimes more likely to see their homes than the animals themselves. Keep an eye out for insects and small creatures such as rabbits, voles and shrews foraging for food.

Mouse-sized shrews eat earthworms that they find under fallen leaves.

Smaller plants grow on the floors of deciduous woods. The trees protect them, while letting through enough sunlight for them to thrive. Look for ferns, flowers and climbing plants such as ivy, which often grow up the trees themselves. You might also see toadstools and other plant-like growths, called fungi.

Ferns

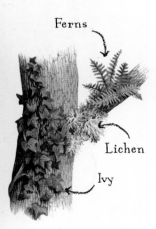

Lichen

Ivy

Primrose

Flowering plants often grow in the shade of the leafy canopy above.

Many broadleaved woods are carpeted with bluebells in the spring.

Conifer critters

A coniferous wood can be dark and dense.
The tall trees block out much of the light
and the ground is often covered with a thick
layer of fallen needles. Fewer animals
and plants live here than in broadleaved
woods, but there's still a lot of wildlife
spotting to do. If you're lucky and patient,
you may see some more unusual sights, too.

Pine martens live in
remote pine woods.

Foxes sometimes
raise their cubs in
coniferous woods.

Long-eared owls come
out at night to hunt.

Spotting woodland wildlife

A good way to explore a wood is to walk slowly
and quietly through it, looking around as you go.
Animals might run or fly away when they hear
you, so it's a good idea to find a convenient spot
and sit there silently for a bit. You won't see
everything at once, so come back regularly.

HANDY HINTS
Wearing clothes
in dull greens or
browns will help you
blend in better with
the scenery. If you
have binoculars, you
could use them to
help you watch birds
in the treetops.

When squirrels gnaw cones, they pull off the scales, eat the seeds and leave a rough stem behind.

A blue tit has chipped away this walnut's hard shell to reach the nut inside.

Beechnut eaten by a woodpecker

After these two hungry mice have finished, there will barely be any horse chestnut left to find.

Signs of life

You would be extremely lucky to enter a wood and see every animal described in this book, but you can easily hunt for clues to tell you that they've been there. These might include nibbled nutshells or cone scales under a tree, feathers, nuts lodged in bark crevices, shredded cones and even bones and droppings.

Leftovers

Most of an animal's day is spent looking for food, and the leftovers of their meals are obvious signs to spot. Every creature tackles its meal in a different way, cracking, tearing, biting, shredding and gnawing their food to pieces. Look out for teethmarks made by mice and squirrels, or neat, smooth-edged holes pecked out by a bird's beak.

Bark and biting

As well as making holes in bark, animals do other things that leave their mark on trees. Small, furry mammals gnaw bark off or use it to sharpen their claws, while deer rub their antlers on it. Mammals often use jagged bark to scratch an itch, leaving tufts of fur behind.

Bank voles strip bark off trees, to eat the soft layer beneath.

Feathered finds

Droppings and feathers are a real giveaway when it comes to finding trees where birds live, although you might find them anywhere in a wood or garden. Some meat-eating birds also spit out the furry, bony remains of their dinners as small, solid pellets. The best place to look for these is under the big old trees where they like to perch. If you find a pellet, you could try taking it to pieces to see what's inside.

Pheasant body feather

Jay wing feather

1. When you find a pellet, use rubber gloves to pick it up, then put it in a bag and take it home.

A barn owl pellet and its contents

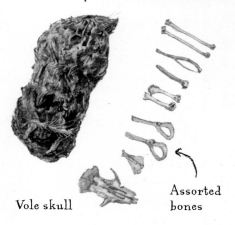

2. Using tweezers, carefully pick it apart and lay out the contents on a sheet of plain paper to look at.

Wood pigeon wing feather

All three feathers above belong to birds that you might find in woodlands.

Vole skull

Assorted bones

Tree pests

Many living things feed on a tree's fruits and nectar, but to some creatures, a tree's sap, leaves and other vital parts offer a more tempting meal. This isn't always a problem. If a tree's leaves are nibbled by insects, it can grow new ones. But some kinds of pests can do more serious damage.

The shape, colour and size of an insect gall depends on the tree and the insect that formed it.

Oak marble gall

Young gall wasp climbing out of hole in gall

Prickly "pineapple" gall

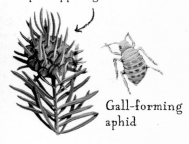

Gall-forming aphid

Cosy eggs

Many insects lay their eggs on trees because they provide a ready source of food when the young larvae hatch. While they are laying their eggs, for example on a leaf or shoot, some types of insect inject it with a chemical. This causes the tree to grow a lump called a gall around the eggs, to protect itself.

Galls also provide shelter and often food, for the larvae. When they are ready, the insects eat their way out. On some galls, you can see an escape hole.

This hazelnut has a side cut away to show a weevil larva growing inside.

Adult nut weevil

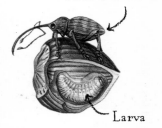

Larva

The different types of galls on this oak leaf were caused by different insects.

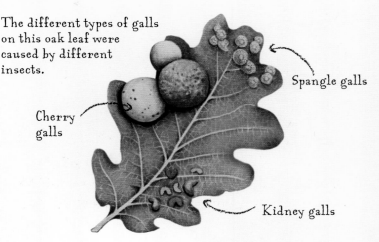

Spangle galls

Cherry galls

Kidney galls

Hungry babies

When insect eggs hatch, the larvae are very hungry. Squiggly marks and holes chewed out of a leaf are signs that it's been hijacked as an insect's dinner. Look out for butterfly and moth caterpillars feeding on trees. Each species mostly lives on one type of tree. So if you look at lots of trees in early summer, you may be able to figure out what eats what.

Some caterpillars, like these sawfly larvae, are a serious problem to trees. Hordes of them can strip a tree bare of its leaves.

These squiggles look like drizzles of paint, but they're not. They're leaf mines, made by burrowing insects eating the leaves from the inside.

This lone moth caterpillar can destroy hundreds of healthy leaves.

Elm bark beetles tunnel under the bark of elm trees, spreading Dutch elm disease from tree to tree as they go.

Tunnels

Elm bark beetle

Adult insects can be as much of a nuisance to a tree as their young, since they tend to be just as greedy. A few carry diseases, too. Dutch elm disease is caused by a fungus, but it is spread from one tree to another by elm bark beetles.

Parasites

Parasites are plants or animals that
attach themselves to other living
things and suck out their juices,
a bit like vampires in horror
stories. Parasites usually
damage the trees they're
feeding from (their hosts),
but they hardly ever kill
them. After all, the hosts
are what keeps them alive.

Mistletoe often grows on apple trees.
It makes some food in its leaves, but
relies on its host for water and
goodness from the soil.

Fungus

Fungus (plural: fungi) is one of the most
serious parasites that can attack a tree.
Fungi have no leaves so they can't make
their own food. Instead, they invade
the heartwood in the middle of a tree
trunk with thousands of tiny threads.
Toadstools (which look like mushrooms)
are one type of fungus. There are others
that look like enormous plates, lumps
of raw meat or blobs of jelly.

These toadstools are clustered at
the base of a fungus-infected tree.

How fungus can kill

If a tree suffers serious damage, such as losing a branch or being struck by lightning, that's when fungus makes its move. Tiny spores (like plant seeds) enter the wound and spread through the trunk, rotting its insides and weakening it or causing the tree to die back. It doesn't matter to fungus whether it kills its host or not, because it grows on dead things as well as living ones.

White pine blister rust is a fungus which causes swellings on pine trunks and branches.

Bracket fungus causes a disease called conifer heart rot. It weakens the inside of the tree, which usually later snaps in the wind.

Dryad's saddle bracket fungus

Cuts and grazes

Trees aren't completely helpless against injury, though. Like your body, a tree can help itself if it's only damaged a little. Look on tree trunks for round, smooth spots. These are sealed-up wounds left behind where a branch has broken off and new wood has grown over.

Recent damage

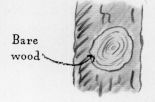

Bare wood

1. When the branch has just broken off, you can see a patch of bare wood, where the branch was. Fungi can easily get in.

Three years later

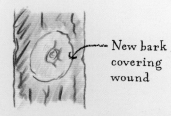

New bark covering wound

2. A new bark layer starts to grow in from the edges. This will gradually grow across and cover the damage.

About six years later

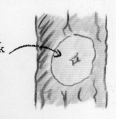

3. A wound on a tree heals very slowly. In an old tree, the bare wood may never be totally covered.

Life in dead trees

With a bit of luck and the right conditions, trees can live for hundreds or, in the odd case, even thousands of years. All through its life a tree sheds branches, leaves and bark. One day, it will die completely. But other plants and animals carry on living in its remains.

Recycling

When a tree dies, fungi and other creatures too tiny to see, get inside and start to break it down. This is called decay, or rotting. Decay is really important in nature because it releases all the raw materials the tree was made from, and puts them back into the soil. These can then be used by new young plants to make them strong.

Crumbling bark and hollow trunks also carry on providing homes for all sorts of creatures. A third of all living things in a wood rely in some way on dead trees to stay alive.

Even though this tree has died, it's still full of life. It has become home to a mass of moss, fungi and hidden insects.

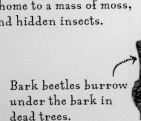

Bark beetles burrow under the bark in dead trees.

58

Leaf litter and wood piles

When deciduous trees shed their leaves in autumn, the dead leaves pile up at the foot of the tree. These piles, known as leaf litter, form a dark and secret world of damp crevices, a haven for creepy-crawlies and other small animals. Lift up some leaves and see what might be lurking underneath. (But put them back afterwards.)

You don't need to visit a wood to see the sorts of animals that hang around tree remains. Arranging a small pile of dead branches or leaves in a shady corner of a garden will encourage animals to visit and plants to grow. Leave the pile undisturbed after you've made it, then watch what moves in.

Stag beetles live in rotting wood.

Grey slugs munch on fresh and rotting leaves.

Dead leaves are a feast for a passing millipede.

All the animals on this page are attracted to moist, shady wood and leaf piles.

Woodlice scuttle around under rotting bark.

Common toad

A rich mix of leaves and fallen berries like this could feed and shelter dozens of tiny creatures.

Trees to spot

In this section of the book, you'll find pictures and descriptions of common trees and winter buds to spot. Each one has facts you might need to know about the tree's mature height, its fruits and flowers, its bark, and where to look for it.

You can find links to more field guides on the Usborne Quicklinks Website at *www.usborne-quicklinks.com*

Monkey puzzle (Chile pine)

Up to 26m (85ft). Overlapping, glossy leaves covering the shoots. Bristly, ball-shaped cone. Gardens and parks.

Conifers

Cones

Lawson cypress

Up to 38m (125ft). Narrow shape. Small, round cones and sprays of scaly leaves. Purple-brown, flaky bark. Often planted as a hedge.

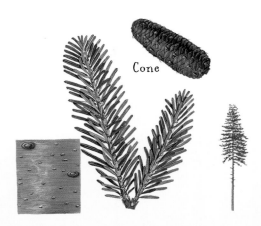

Cone

European silver fir

Up to 48m (157ft). Large, upright cones at top of tree. Flat needles have silver underside. Flat, round scars left on twigs when needles drop. Woods.

Berry-like cone

Yew

Up to 20m (66ft). Male and female flowers usually on separate trees. Smooth, flaking bark. Young cones are green. Woods, churchyards.

Young cone

Adult cone

Western hemlock

Up to 48m (157ft). Drooping branches and top shoots. Reddish flowers and small, brown cones. Needles various lengths. Woods.

Cone

Norway spruce

Up to 45m (148ft). Long, hanging cones and sharp, rigid needles. Reddish flowers. Commonly used as Christmas trees. Parks, gardens, woods.

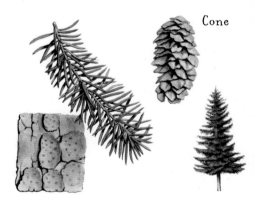

Cone

Sitka spruce

Up to 47m (154ft). Long, hanging cones. Very prickly needles. Fat, yellow buds on yellow twigs. Bark flakes off in "plates". Parks, coasts, woods.

Juniper

Up to 6m (20ft). Sharp needles arranged in threes. Berry-like cones turn purplish in second year. Often grows as a shrub. Open spaces.

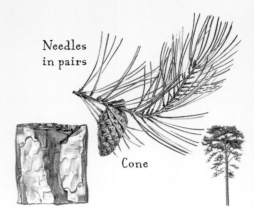

Scots pine

Up to 35m (115ft). Small, pointed buds. Bark is red near top of tree, becoming grey below, peels in odd shapes. Mountains and sandy soil.

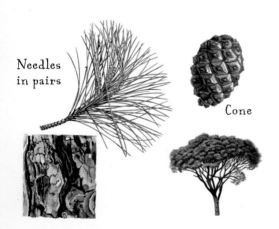

Stone pine

Up to 22m (72ft). Long, stiff, paired needles. Small buds. Green cones turn brown with age. Deeply ridged bark. Mediterranean coast.

Monterey pine

Up to 30m (98ft). Slender, grass-green needles growing in threes. Dumpy cones stay on tree for many years. Near the coast.

Atlas cedar

Up to 40m (131ft). Large, spreading tree with barrel-shaped cones. Blue-green or dark green needles grow singly or in rosettes. Woods and parks.

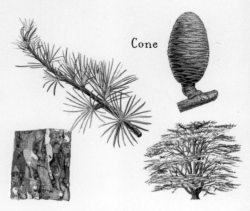

Cedar of Lebanon

Up to 40m (131ft). Leaves can grow singly or in dense clusters. Yellow flowers. Cones like Atlas cedar, but without flattened top. Parks.

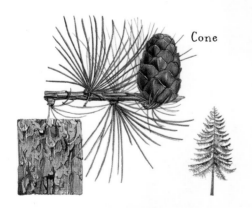

European larch

Up to 45m (148ft). Rosettes of soft needles turn yellow then fall off in winter. Drooping yellow male flowers, red female flowers. Widespread.

Japanese larch

Up to 37m (121ft). Cones have unusual folded edges. Dark orange-red twigs and pinkish flowers. Blue-green needles fall off in winter. Widespread.

Broadleaves

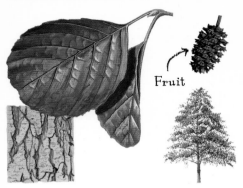

Fruit

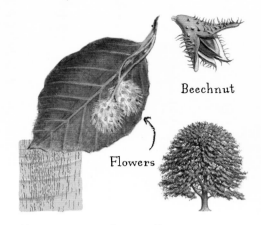

Beechnut

Flowers

Common alder

Up to 25m (82ft). Catkins in early spring. Cone-like fruits which stay on in winter. Greyish-black, scaly bark. Near water and damp woods.

Common beech

Up to 36m (118ft). Smooth, grey bark. Young leaves light green, but become darker. Fruit has woody husk split into four. Widespread.

Fruit

Fruits

Crab apple

Up to 10m (33ft). Five-petalled blossoms appear in May-June. Smallish yellow fruits edible, but sour. Wild in hedges and thickets.

Wild cherry (gean)

Up to 20m (66ft). Reddish-brown bark peels in ribbons. Large white flower clusters appear in spring. Woods and thickets.

Japanese cherry

Up to 20m (66ft). Pink blossoms
appear April-May. Purple-brown
or greyish bark. Many varieties.
Gardens and along streets.

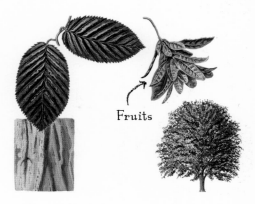

Fruits

Hornbeam

Up to 20m (66ft). Green, winged
fruits hanging in clusters. Brown
(male) and green (female) catkins.
Smooth, grey bark. Hedges, streets.

Fruits

Whitebeam

Up to 25m (82ft). Leaves white and
fuzzy underneath. Grey bark cracks
with age. Five-petalled flowers in
May-June. Sour berries. Grows wild.

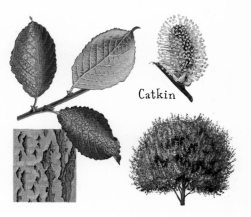

Catkin

Goat or pussy willow

Up to 10m (33ft). Silvery-grey
upright catkins in late winter.
Separate male and female trees.
Hedges and damp woods.

Fruits

Common lime

Up to 40m (131ft). Scented yellow
flowers attract bees in June. Young
bark smooth and grey, ridged when
older. Parks and gardens.

Catkin

Silver birch

Up to 30m (98ft). Pale bark
peels in ribbons. "Lamb's tail"
catkins in April. Wild on heaths and
mountains, also planted in gardens.

Catkin

Crack willow

Up to 15m (49ft). Often has more
than one trunk. Bluish-grey bark,
heavily cracked. Leaves are green on
top, silver underneath. Near water.

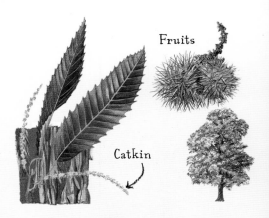

Fruits

Catkin

Sweet chestnut

Up to 35m (115ft). Young bark grey
and smooth. Often spiral patterns on
trunk. Small yellow flowers on long
catkins. Nuts in very prickly green cases.

Laburnum

Up to 7m (23ft). Yellow flowers
in May-June. Greenish-brown bark
becomes less smooth with age.
Poisonous seeds. Gardens.

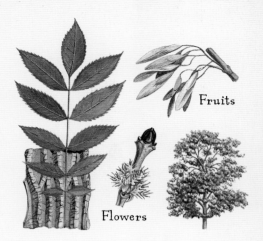

Common ash

Up to 45m (148ft). Grey-brown,
smooth bark, becomes furrowed
with age. Clusters of seeds stay on in
winter. Common in woods and parks.

Rowan (mountain ash)

Up to 20m (66ft). White flowers
in May, followed by red berries in
September. Smooth, shiny grey bark.
Wild on mountains.

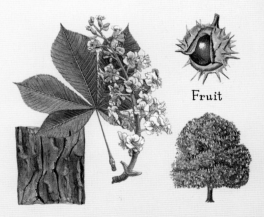

Horse chestnut

Up to 38m (125ft). Horseshoe-shaped
scars left on twigs by fallen leaves.
Flowers in May. Prickly fruits with
conkers inside. Woods and parks.

Fruit

London plane

Up to 45m (148ft). Flaky bark which leaves behind white patches. Flowers have no petals. Spiky, round fruits stay on in winter. City streets.

Lower leaves are less lobed.

White poplar

Up to 26m (85ft). Leaves covered with white down underneath. Whitish-grey bark with diamond-shaped marks. Wet areas, open and waste land.

Fruits

Field maple

Up to 26m (85ft). Tiny green flowers in clusters. Narrow-ridged grey bark. Leaves turn golden in autumn. Hedges and woods.

Fruits

Norway maple

Up to 27m (89ft). Dome-shaped crown. Forms yellow-green flowers in spring. Colourful autumn leaves. Parks, streets and gardens.

Fruit

Sycamore

Up to 35m (115ft). Smooth bark flakes off in large, flat pieces. Winged fruits, called keys, in pairs. Green flowers. Parks and streets.

Berries are called haws.

Hawthorn

Up to 10m (33ft). Thorny twigs. Pinkish-brown bark cracks in oblongs. Small, white flowers in May, berries in autumn. Widespread. Hedges.

Fruit

Sessile oak

Up to 21m (69ft). Dark green, long-stalked leaves. Acorns often stalkless. Grey-brown bark with knobbly ridges. Woods and parks.

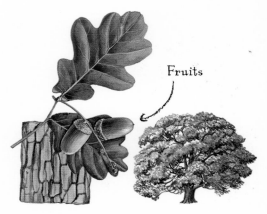

Fruits

English oak

Up to 37m (121ft). Wide-spreading branches. Yellow dangly male catkins. Tiny female flowers on end of new shoots. Common alone and in woods.

Winter twig guide

In winter, when many trees have no leaves or flowers,
you can often use twigs and buds to identify a tree.
Here are some easy questions you could ask yourself:

- What colour are the buds and the twig?
- What shape is the twig?
- Are the buds pointed or rounded?
- How are the buds arranged on the twig?
- Are the buds covered in hair, or scales?
- Are they sticky?
- What shape are the leaf scars?

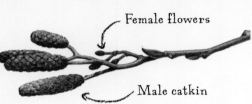

Female flowers

Male catkin

False acacia

Grey twig. Thorns next to tiny,
alternate buds.

Common alder

Alternate, stalked, purple buds,
often with male catkins.

Ash

Smooth, grey twig. Large, black
opposite buds. Leaf scars have a
smile-shaped row of dots.

Beech

Slender twig. Alternate, spiky,
brown buds sticking out.

Wild cherry

Large, glossy, red buds grouped
at tip and along twig.

Sweet chestnut

Knobbly twig. Large, reddish,
alternate buds.

English elm

Zigzag twig. Alternate,
blackish-red buds.

Turkey oak

Clusters of alternate buds
with twisted whiskers.

Magnolia

Huge, furry, green-grey buds.

Common lime

Zigzag twig. Alternate, reddish
buds with two scales.

White poplar

Twig and alternate buds covered
with white down.

London plane

Alternate, cone-shaped buds.
Leaf scars surround the buds.

Willow

Slender twig. Alternate buds
close to twig.

Sycamore

Large, green, opposite buds with
dark-edged scales. Pale leaf scars.

Whitebeam

Downy, green, alternate buds.

Walnut

Thick, hollow twig. Heart-shaped leaf
scars. Black, velvety alternate buds.

The pictures below show the different cuts of wood that come from this log.

Working with wood

Ever since the first caveman ate a fruit or rubbed sticks together to make fire, people have used trees for all sorts of things: to make boats, houses, furniture, tools, ornaments, medicines, foods and paper. For some people, trees are an important part of religion, too.

Wide planks come from the sides, or all the wood is mashed up to make paper.

From tree to timber

Before a tree can be made into anything, it has to be cut down. Years ago, this was a back-breaking job done with an axe, but modern machines make light work of it. The branches are sliced off the felled tree, then the trunk is cut into logs and taken to a sawmill. A log can be sawn into planks of many sizes, or made into wood chips or pulp.

Wood is full of moisture, so freshly cut planks need drying out, or seasoning, before they can be used. This is done by piling them like a stack of waffles and leaving them in the open air, or drying them in a type of oven called a kiln.

Heartwood makes strong timber for building.

The bark is mashed into wood chips.

Stacking planks with gaps between allows the air to flow around them.

Patterns and marks

When a plank is cut from a log, the annual rings make a pattern of wavy or straight lines called the grain. Wood cut along the grain is stronger than wood cut across it. Round or eye-shaped marks called knots in the wood show where a branch joined the trunk.

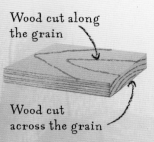

Wood cut along the grain

Wood cut across the grain

You can count the rings in a knot to see how old the branch that made it was.

Knot

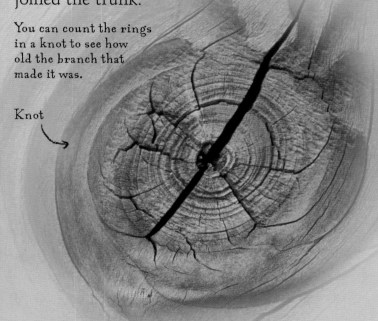

Section of trunk cut along the grain

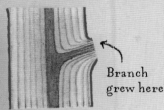

Branch grew here

The picture above shows the type of trunk that would have created the knot on the left.

Hardwood and softwood

The wood that comes from broadleaves and conifers is as different as the trees themselves. Conifer wood, called softwood, is used more than hardwood from broadleaved trees, because it grows in more regular shapes and it's easier to cut. Even so, there are many trees of both types that have especially useful wood.

DID YOU KNOW?

Wood isn't the only useful thing that comes from trees. A chemical in willow bark was the source of aspirin. Certain buds are dried and used as cooking spices. Even amber and rubber are tree products – made from sap.

A world without trees

Trees do so many important things that a world without them would probably be a world without animals or people, either – a sick, filthy, parched wasteland.

These woodland butterflies were once common in Britain, but are now endangered or extinct.

High brown fritillary (endangered)

Swallowtails (endangered)

Every year, all over the world, vast areas of trees are destroyed accidentally by fires, deliberately cut down for timber, or cleared to make space for farming. When this happens, many animals lose their homes and many die.

The ones that survive might move to new areas, but then they have to compete for food with the animals that already live there. So life just gets harder and harder. The unluckiest animals just can't survive the change, and may eventually die out altogether.

Large blue (extinct)

Large tortoiseshell (extinct)

DID YOU KNOW?
Experts think that up to 50,000 rainforest plant and animal species die out every year, as their homes are torn down or burned. The last time living things died out so fast was when dinosaurs existed.

Water crisis

With fewer trees, water supplies start to become dank and muddy. During storms, trees' roots normally help to control the speed at which rainwater flows into streams. But, without them, floods soon wash the top layer of soil away into rivers and streams, suffocating the fish and making the water too dirty to drink.

Choking and frying

As trees continue to disappear, so does the oxygen, which the leaves produced. The leaves also filtered out smoke, dust and ash from vehicles and factories, keeping the air clear and clean. When the trees are gone, the thin, stale air will slowly fill up with dirt and grime.

And, if that wasn't bad enough, the world will probably get hotter, too. When plants make food, they use carbon dioxide gas from the air. The remaining carbon dioxide helps to trap heat from the Sun, keeping the Earth comfortably warm enough for life to exist. But without trees to help keep this balance, too much carbon dioxide might build up in the air, allowing less and less heat to escape. This would make the whole planet heat up like an oven.

But the story doesn't have to end like this...

Trees use carbon dioxide gas from the air. Heat that came from the Sun can escape to keep Earth's temperature just right for living things.

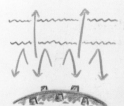

When trees are cut down, more carbon dioxide stays in the air. It traps more heat, warming the Earth like a greenhouse on a hot day.

  Heat

⁓⁓⁓ Carbon dioxide

With modern technology, people can cut down trees quicker than ever.

Making a difference

Everyone can do their bit to protect trees and make sure they live to continue doing good things in the future. The easiest way to do this is to treat them with respect. When it comes to nature, "Look but don't touch" is a good thing to remember.

If you find a tree that interests you, don't pull bits off – the tree needs them more than you do. Just looking at a tree will usually tell you quite a lot about it. For an even closer view, try hunting for pieces it has shed on the ground.

Make sure your family and friends know about the dangers of lighting campfires and barbecues, or smoking cigarettes, near woods or dry grasses and shrubs. Wood fires are very hard to control. With a little help from the wind, they can turn acres of trees into a desert of smouldering ashes in a few hours.

Leaves, fruits and seeds often fall off a tree, giving you an ideal opportunity to have a really close look.

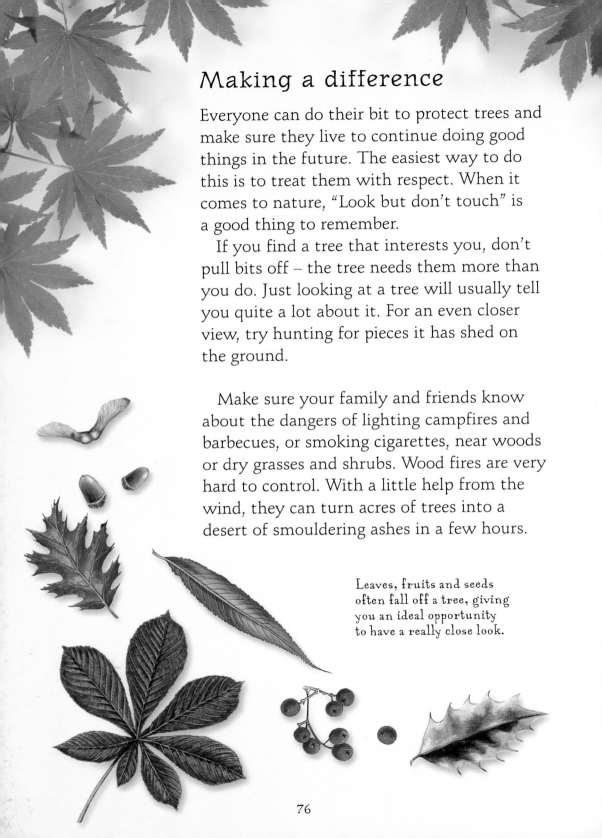

Going further

From time to time there are stories in the news about people who sit in trees to make sure they don't get cut down, but there are other, simpler ways to help protect and preserve trees.

Re-using and recycling paper in your home, and encouraging recycling at school or work, helps reduce the number of trees that need to be cut down to make new things. Try to use products labelled "sustainable" (like this book). This means that for every tree cut down to make it, new ones are planted to replace it.

Another great way to help the natural world, if you want to go a step further, is by planting a tree yourself. You might not have a garden big enough to do this, but there are lots of organizations you can join which are involved with tree planting. There are even companies that will plant a tree in a wood for you, as a gift to another person.

If enough people did something to help, however small, it could make a big difference both for the future of trees, and for the future of the planet.

HANDY HINTS
This symbol on cardboard means it can be recycled.

The more people get involved in tree-planting schemes, the more likely fragile pine saplings like these are to grow into huge, dense forests.

Glossary

Here are some words in the book you might not know. Any word in *italics* is defined elsewhere in the glossary.

Annual ring A ring of dark and light wood in the cross-section of a *trunk* or branch that shows one year's growth

Bark A tough outer layer that protects the tree's insides

Blossom *Flowers*

Bract A leaf-like part of a cone supporting the *seed*

Broadleaved tree (broadleaf) A tree that has wide, flat leaves. Most are *deciduous*.

Bud An undeveloped *shoot*, leaf or *flower*

Bud scale scar A ring-shaped mark around a twig, left when the *terminal bud scales (2)* fall off

Cambium A thin layer that produces new *inner bark* and *sapwood* in a tree *trunk*

Catkin An often sausage-shaped cluster of tiny *flowers*, all of the same sex, growing on one stalk

Chlorophyll A green chemical found in leaves that absorbs sunlight to help make food for the plant

Compound leaf A type of leaf made up of smaller *leaflets*

Cones The *fruits* of *conifers*

Conifer A tree with needle-like or scaly leaves, which bear *cones* with their seeds inside. Most are *evergreen*.

Crown A tree's branches, twigs and leaves

Cutting A part of a tree, such as a *shoot* or *root*, cut off and used to grow a new tree

Deciduous Losing its leaves over a few weeks, usually in autumn

Entire leaf A leaf that has a smooth edge

Evergreen Losing its leaves throughout the year, so the tree is always green

Fertilization The joining of an *ovule* with *pollen* to make a *seed*

Flowers The parts of a tree where new *seeds* are made

Fruits The parts of a tree that hold its *seeds*.

Heartwood Old wood at the core of the *trunk* that has grown too solid to carry water

Inner bark A layer beneath the outer layer of *bark* that grows every year

Leaflets Leaf-like sections that make up a *compound leaf*

Leaf scar Mark left on a twig where a leaf has fallen off

Leaf skeleton The dried-up remainder of a leaf

Lobed leaf A type of leaf or *leaflet*, partly divided into sections called lobes

Nectar A sweet, sticky liquid produced by *flowers* to attract insects

Ovary A female part of a *flower* that contains *ovules*

Ovule A plant "egg"

Pollen A powder made by the *flower's* male parts for transfer to the female parts to make *seeds*

Rootlet The smallest of *roots*

Roots Parts of a tree that grow into the ground, absorbing water and goodness from the soil and anchoring the tree

Sap A liquid that carries sugars (food made in the leaves) around the tree

Sapwood The outer area of wood in a tree *trunk* that carries water up from the *roots* to the rest of the tree

Scales (1) The tough, woody parts of a *cone* (2) A *bud's* outer layers

Seed Grows from a fertilized *ovule*, and may eventually form a new plant

Seedling A very young tree that has grown from a *seed*

Sepals Leaf-like parts that protect *buds*

Shoot A young stem or twig bearing leaves

Simple leaf A type of leaf that is all in one piece

Stamen The male part of a *flower*, where *pollen* is made

Terminal bud A *bud* at the tip of a shoot or twig

Timber Wood, especially when harvested

Toothed leaf A leaf or *leaflet* with jagged edges

Trunk The main woody stem of the tree that holds it upright

Variegated A type of leaf that has two or more colours

Veins Tiny tubes inside a leaf that carry water to all parts of the leaf and carry food away from it

Index

Acknowledgements

Every effort has been made to trace the copyright holders of material in this book. If any rights have been omitted, the publishers offer to rectify this in any subsequent editions following notification. The publishers are grateful to the following organizations and individuals for their permission to reproduce material:

Cover © blickwinkel/Alamy; **1** © Frederic Didillon/OSF; **p2-3** © Tim Gartside/Alamy; **p4-5** © Pearson Victoria/OSF; **p6-7** © Digital Vision; **p8** © PCL/Alamy; **p10** © Royalty-Free/Corbis; **p13** © Nigel Cattlin/FLPA; **p17** © Wegner/ARCO/naturepl.com; **p19** © Digital Vision; **p21** © Owen Franken/CORBIS; **p23** © Cambridge2000.com; **p25** © Christopher Barnes/Alamy; **p26** © Den Reader/Alamy; **p30** © Jan Vermeer/Foto Natura/FLPA; **p33** © Brand X Pictures/Alamy; **p34** © Michael Marten/Science Photo Library; **p37** © Aflo/Naturepl.com; **p39** © artpartner-images.com/Alamy; **p43** © Michael Piazza/OSF; **p44** © Duncan Usher/Ardea London Ltd; **p46** © Photowood Inc./CORBIS; **p49** © NHPA/Alan Williams; **p52** © Lothar Lenz/zefa/Corbis; **p55** © Leroy Simon/Visuals Unlimited/Getty Images; **p56** © imagebroker/Alamy; **p58** © blickwinkel/Alamy; **p61** © Marc Grimberg/Alamy; **p62** © Digital Vision; **p63** © Digital Vision; **p64** © Bloom Works Inc./Alamy; **p65** © Keith Douglas/Alamy

Illustrators

Dave Ashby, Mike Atkinson, Graham Austin, Bob Bampton, John Barber, Andrew Beckett, Joyce Bee, Isabel Bowring, Trevor Boyer, Wendy Bramall, Maggie Brand, Paul Brooks, Peter Bull, Mark Burgess, Hilary Burn, Sue Camm, Kuo Kang Chen, Roger H Coggins, Frankie Coventry, Christine Darter, Kate Davies, Sarah De Ath, Kevin Dean, Peter Dennis, Michelle Emblem, Sandra Fernandez, Denise Finney, Sarah Fox-Davies, John Francis, Nigel Frey, Sheila Galbraith, William Giles, Victoria Gooman, Victoria Gordon, Coral Guppy, Laura Hammonds, Alan Harris, Tim Hayward, Christine Howes, David Hurrell, Ian Jackson, Roger Kent, Aziz Khan, Colin King, Steven Kirk, Richard Lewington, Ken Lily, Mick Loates, Rachel Lockwood, Kevin Lyles, Chris Lyon, Alan Male, Andy Martin, Uwe Mayer, Rob McCaig, Joseph McEwan, Malcom McGregor, Caroline McLean, Dee McLean, Richard Millington, Annabel Milne, David More, Dee Morgan, Tricia Newell, Barbara Nicholson, David Palmer, Charles Pearson, Liz Pepperell, Julie Piper, Gillian Platt, Maurice Pledger, Cynthia Pow, David Quinn, John Shackell, Chris Shields, Maggie Silver, Guy Smith, Peter Stebbing, Ralph Stobart, Sue Testar, Sam Thompson, Sally Voke, Phil Weare, James Wood.

Cover design by: Helen Wood
Digital manipulation by Keith Furnival and Will Dawes
With thanks to Hazel Maskell and Tori Large
Series editor: Jane Chisholm